Sibyls and Others

By the same author

Poems
Cages
To See the Matter Clearly
The Region's Violence
Twenty One Poems
Another Full Moon

Play
All Citizens are Soldiers
(translation from Lope de Vega) – with Alan Sillitoe

Stories
Daylife and Nightlife

Sibyls and Others
Ruth Fainlight

Hutchinson
London Melbourne Sydney Auckland Johannesburg

Hutchinson & Co. (Publishers) Ltd
An imprint of the Hutchinson Publishing Group
3 Fitzroy Square, London W1P 6JD

Hutchinson Group (Australia) Pty Ltd
30–32 Cremorne Street, Richmond South, Victoria 3121
PO Box 151, Broadway, New South Wales 2007

Hutchinson Group (NZ) Ltd
32–34 View Road, PO Box 40-086, Glenfield, Auckland 10

Hutchinson Group (SA) (Pty) Ltd
PO Box 337, Bergvlei 2012, South Africa

First published 1980

© Ruth Fainlight 1980

Set in VIP Bembo by
D. P. Media Limited, Hitchin, Hertfordshire

Printed by the Anchor Press Ltd
and bound by Wm Brendon & Son Ltd
both of Tiptree, Essex

British Library Cataloguing in Publication Data

Fainlight, Ruth
  Sibyls and others.
  I. Title
  821'.9'14   PS3556.A35A17

ISBN 0-09-141030 4

To
LB & BH

ACKNOWLEDGEMENTS

Some of these poems were first published by:
*Annalog, Bananas, European Judaism, Gallery,
The Honest Ulsterman, Hudson Review, In 'hui, The
Jewish Chronicle, The Literary Review, Massachusetts
Review, Meridian, The Nation, New Poems 76–77,
New Poetry nos. 2, 3, 5 – Arts Council of Great Britain,
The New Review, New Statesman, Ontario Review,
Other Poetry, Outposts, PEN Broadsheet no. 6, PN
Review, Poetry Dimension no. 5, Proteus, The Saturday
Night Reader, Sceptre Press, The Scotsman, Southern
Review, Spirit, Studia Mystica, Times Literary
Supplement, TR, Voices Within the Ark, Avon Books.*
Illustration by Leonard Baskin is reproduced by
kind permission of the artist.

Contents

Sibyls
A Sibyl	13
Aeneas' Meeting with the Sibyl	14
A Desert Sibyl	16
The Cumaean Sibyl I	17
The Cumaean Sibyl II	18
From The Sibylline Books	19
The Hebrew Sibyl	20
Sibyl of the Waters	21
The Delphic Sibyl	22
Destruction of a Sibyl	23
Herophile	25
Sibyl on the Run	26
Hallucinating Sibyl	27
The Cimmerian Sibyl	29
Sick Sibyl	31
Blocked Sibyl	32
Rescue of the Sibyl	33
The Persian Sibyl	35
The Sibyls in Amiens Cathedral	36
The Sibila	38
The Libyan Sibyl	39
The Phrygian Sibyl	40
The Shinto Sibyl	41
The Tiburtine Sibyl	42
The Oracle at Dodona	43
A Young Sibyl	44
Introspection of a Sibyl	46

Others
Only the Magpie	51
Time's Metaphors	52

Danger Areas	53
Driving Northward	54
The Route Napoleon	55
Trees	56
Deadheading the Roses	57
The New Tree	58
Weeds	59
Without Naomi	60
New Year in England	62
The First of October	63
The Daisy Chain	64
With David in the Nimrud Galleries	66
Childhood	68
The Message	69
A Child Crying	70
Almost-Full Moon	71
That Smile	72
Domestical	74
It Must	76
Anja's Poem	78
Divination by Hair	80
Wisdom of the Mothers	84
Satellite	85
Meeting	87
Again	88
Animal Tamer	89
Any Old Couple	90
Going Back	91
The Function of Tears	92
Suddenly	95
Grief	96
Not Well-Mapped as Heaven	97

The Thorn	98
My Rings	99
Questions	101
Not Grief but Fear	102
Commemorated	104
Too Late	105
Time Come	106
Terra Incognita	107
That Coming Mystery	108
Fire	109
All Those Victorian Paintings	110
Belief	111
Evening and Dawn	112
Summer Storm	114
Midsummer Night	115
Squirrel in Holland Park	116
Hospital Flowers	117
House-Guest	119
The Gambler	120
Always Time	122
Dreaming	124
Sweet Solitude	126
Usually Dry-Eyed	127
Country Lady	128
Meat	130
Aftermath	132
The King Must Die	134
The New Science of Strong Materials	136
A Poem	138
Two Cripples	139
The Dancing Floor	140

sibyls

A Sibyl

Her eyes have an indrawn look,
like a bird hatching its eggs.
To whose voice is she listening?
Anxious, the questioners, waiting
those words, but she seems relaxed
and calm, turning the leaves
of her book, does not even
glance down before her finger
points the message: this cave
familiar as a nest,
and she, its rightful tenant –
no longer forced to make
a choice between two worlds.

Aeneas' Meeting with the Sibyl

Hunched over rustling leaves spread out
before her on the stony ground, like a skinny
gypsy with a joint dripping ash in the corner of her mouth
quizzing the Tarot cards, pulling the shabby
shawl closer round elbows and shoulders, then squinting
shrewdly sideways up at a nervous client,
the sibyl greeted Aeneas. 'Don't tell it from them,'
he pleaded. She was sitting cross-legged, right at the door
of her cave, and he'd heard how often the wind (Apollo!
he thought, it's draughty here, no wonder she looks
so pinched and cold), shuffled the leaves into total
confusion, which she didn't seem to notice or
amend. 'Don't show them to me. Say it in words.'

'You're all the same,' she grumbled. 'Always wanting
more than you pay for. Of course' – tilting her head
sideways on that mole-strewn stringy neck
(he saw white hairs among her dusty curls),
an inappropriate cajoling smile –
distorting her archaic features – 'if you give
me something extra,' she wheedled, 'I'll do you a special.'
The tattered russet-purple layers of skin
and cloth wrapped around her body dispersed
an ancient odour of sweat or incense as her movements
stirred them. Through a hole in the skirt he glimpsed a lean
and sinewy thigh, and feet bound up in rags.
'Come inside, young man,' she ordered. 'We'll be private
    there.'

Remembering what came next: his search for the golden
bough, their descent into Hades, the twittering shades,
his painful meeting with Dido, the Sibyl's answer
to Palinurus, and then, at last,
what he'd wanted: embracing Anchises his father, and
    learning
the destiny of their descendants, the future
of Rome; Aeneas found it hard to reconcile
his first impressions with the awesome, powerful figure
who led him safely through the realm of death
and to the daylight world again. He looked
back from the shore to where she crouched outside
her cave, waiting for another questioner –
and saw she had assumed the same disguise.

A Desert Sibyl

A ranting, middle-aged albino,
gaunt and sharp-featured, a desert sibyl,
open-mouthed, eyes blurring, sightless;

who journeyed through the parching dunes
and past the heights of Mount Tibesti;
up from Lake Chad with her sacred ibis;

intent that all should hear her message –
verses Tanit's power inspired:
warning for Dido, queen of Carthage.

The Cumaean Sibyl I

She was the one who, three by three,
burned her books of prophesy
when the asking price would not be met.
Like a wise old nurse who knows that children
rage and fret, but when night comes,
creep back into her arms, she watched
the flames, abstracted, stern, and calm.

Her face seemed veiled, the net of lines
a mask, a zone of darker air,
penumbra of another atmosphere –
as though she stood before a fire
deep in her cave, brooding upon
time past and still to come, far from
this splendour and destruction.

Tarquinius Superbus gasped
and broke the silence. 'I'll pay your price.
More than my nurse or mother, sibyl,
is your worth to me – your prophesies
and wisdom.' 'The same price as for all
the nine.' 'Agreed.' She raised her hand,
the fire died, the last three books were saved.

The Cumaean Sibyl II

Because she forgot to ask for youth
when Apollo gave her as many years
as grains of dust in her hand, this sibyl
personifies old age: and yet
those withered breasts can still let down
celestial milk to one who craves
redemption: a dry tree, not a green,
the emblem of salvation.

From 'The Sibylline Books'
(book V. verses 512–530)

Threatening every star, I saw the sun's gleaming
   sword-blade,
the moon's rage between lightning flashes. The stars
   were at war:
God allowed the fight. For instead of the sun, flames
thrust from the east like searching beams of light, and
   stopped
the two-faced revolution of the moon's changes.

Lucifer fought hard, mounted on Leo's back.
Wily Capricorn attacked young Taurus; with murderous
razor horns, bull and goat bled out their future.
Orion smashed the Scales; Virgo and Gemini
invaded Mars. The bright Pleiades vanished. Draco
surrendered the Buckle and Belt, Pisces overthrew
the realm of Leo: in dread of whom, Scorpio destroyed
himself with his poisoned tail. Armoured Cancer fled,
scuttling away from the whirling club of Orion, the
   hunter.
Sirius, dog-star, succumbed, vanquished by the sun's
   heat;
Aquarius consumed by ardent Lucifer.

Heaven itself was stirred at last to fiery wrath.
Horizon to zenith, the firmament shook, stunning the
   warriors,
plunging them headlong down into Ocean's waters.
The hissing trail of their fall kindled the whole earth:
the sky remained starless, all constellations darkened.

The Hebrew Sibyl

I who was driven mad and cast out
from the high walls of Syrian Babylon;
I who announced the fire of God's anger;
who prophesy to those about to die
divine riddles,
am still God's oracle.

Mortals in Hellas will claim me,
name me as from another city of birth –
Erythrae – one of the shameless.
Others will say I had an unknown father,
and my mother was Circe –
brand me a crazy impostor.

But when all has taken place,
when the walls collapse and the Tower crumbles –
that coming time, when knowledge is lost
and men no longer understand each other,
no one will call me insane –
but God's great sibyl.

Sibyl of the Waters

Noah's daughter
sibyl of the waters

first sibyl
the most ancient

with Shem, Ham and Japhet
saw her father naked

already she had prophesied
the flood

and understood
it was the nakedness of God.

Arms raised in invocation
officiating at the altar

where the Ark had grated
upon Ararat

she placed the burning brands
shielding her face –

ominous oracular gesture –
then crushed the dove to death

against her breast:
propitiation.

The Delphic Sibyl

The tripod, the laurel leaves, the robe and style
of a virgin, though I was an honest widow of fifty:
because of my sober gaze and my docility,
the elders of Delphi chose me and taught me
what had to be done with the tripod and laurel leaves.
They offered a drink from the holy stream, showed me
the cleft in the rock where I must sit and breathe
mephitic fumes and chew the leaves until
my head began to swim and words came blurred.
Those gentlemen of Delphi's best, most ancient
families, our city's noble priests,
quite overwhelmed me. I was a simple woman,
obedient, eager to please, and honoured
by the role. And even had I wanted
to, been bribed to do, there was no chance
to slant the augeries. Petitioners
would proffer written questions first to them,
and their interpretations of my drugged
and mumbled ravings were determined by
Apollo's demands and the city's political needs.
I was an ideal oracle, they told me.
Thus I grew old, though monthly more confused,
appalled, exhausted, and in every way
the opposite of all I once assumed.

Destruction of a Sibyl

Right from the start, the Pythia was depressed.
Every omen came unfavourable.
He'd been on duty at the sanctuary, and
afterwards, telling his friend Plutarch
about the catastrophe, Nicander, one
of the priests at Delphi, could still remember her
  screams.

She'd gone into the proper trance, but how
reluctantly; at once began to speak
in a strange, hoarse voice. Whatever dumb and evil
spirit had possessed her would not reveal
its origin. No curse the priests pronounced could
banish it, protect her or themselves.

Like a ship on a stormy sea, foundering,
when bales of precious cargo are jettisoned
and the galley-slaves pull harder and faster because
of the lash, though their oars have splintered, she lurched
and shuddered, struggling to escape; tried to crawl
on bleeding hands and knees toward the door.

That cowardice could never be purged. No matter
how long they lived, the whole College of Priests
would not forget the shame. Everyone fled.
Contagion of fear: panic alone had ruled.
Apollo's priests abandoned their oracle,
and when they returned, found her broken and changed.

Python uncoiled himself, in all the glistening
length of his body, come back to remind them of
the ancient goddess, the Mother Apollo usurped.
It was She who had spoken and claimed the soul
of the Pythia to serve at Her altar and be
Her oracle forever in the underworld.

Herophile

Whenever she stopped at Delphi, Herophile,
the oldest sibyl, would stand on a special rock
and chant her oracle. Long before Helen
was born, she had foretold the girl would grow up
a trouble-maker, the bane of Europe and Asia.

Through forests and over mountains she wandered,
    but two
towns wrangled for the honour of her birth:
Marpessus the red (whose thirsty soil swallows
the river Aidoneus), and Erythrae.

Sometimes the sibyl said her mother had been
a nymph, an immortal; at others named herself daughter
or bride to Apollo – Artemis, his sister and twin.

When Herophile finally died, her tomb was built
by a stream in his temple grove – Apollo Smintheus,
he who protects the crops, destroying mice
that plague the ripening fields – and guarded by
a stony herm whose blankness seemed to mock
a life of traveller's alarms; poor food;
the sight of too much human misery,
hope and credulity and ceremony;
bad roads; virginity; and solitude.

Sibyl on the Run

Vague gaze from tired grey eyes
under the wide brim of her hat,
the fine-grained white skin of her face
mud-splashed, hair tangled, uncurling,

harried by wind and rain, she creeps
through the door of the smoky hut, and quick
as a snake, wary and furtive as
a forest animal, thrusts out
a scratched hand to take one of
the oat-cakes from the hearth, crumbles it
into her mouth, gulping with haste –

looks round the silent circle of watchers
(no need to doubt, these were believers);
then reassured, straightens her back,
raises her chin, loosens her ragged cloak,
arrogant and proud; announces
herself: the wisest sibyl on earth.

Hallucinating Sibyl

As though burning upwards –
her waxy flesh become
candle to the flame of Apollo,
entirely possessed –
sibyl of Thrace,
sister of Pythagoras,
hallucinating sibyl.

Flakes of snow swirl and
drift through the cave mouth.
Eddies of wind
intensify the glow.
The brands throb
like the heart still beating between
the split rib-cage of the sacrifice.

Entranced before the fire,
open-mouthed, throat and chest
reflecting light like a breast-plate,
naked shoulders shadowed
and glinting eyes rolled white
to see armies clashing,
phalanxes in the heavens

above the roof of the cave:
her mantic vision penetrates
through rocks, earth, roots
of winter-stripped trees,
the turbulent heavy sky
that shrouds the land
from the Euxine sea to the Hellespont.

Further back, beyond
the circle of light, the influence
of its noisome, pungent
fumes, stand priests
with the dagger and bowl for the blood
she drinks, the skins to clothe her
after she has prophesied.

Candle to the flame of Apollo,
entirely possessed;
sibyl of Thrace,
sister of Pythagoras,
sibyl hallucinating –
but not yet begun
to use Apollo's words or speak with his voice.

The Cimmerian Sibyl

These habits come from the old place –
customs brought from home: almost
the only memories of endless
trees, a northern waste of cold
and dark beyond the Caucasus.

Because it was always so, here
on the shores of the Hellespont I still
must have my drum and lance, the three
mushrooms and sacred feathers, before
I rise to heaven and touch the stars.

Everything I know was taught
by the last sibyl able to
recall those days. Crippled, toothless,
and blind, she told me tales of how
we fled the Scythians, and ravaged Thrace.

I learned the steps of the magic dance
(my body burned in trance, the music's
beat made me gulp gallons of water
to quench such thirst); got by heart
the words that trap the reluctant god.

He slides under my skin as smoothly
as the blade of a knife in the hand of one
who slits the pelt and pours warm blood
from the throat of a perfect sacrifice.
Does god or sibyl then pronounce?

But now we are too near Greece, and priests
interpret my oracles, move
between me and the god, stifle my power,
altering the ritual;
fearful; changing the old ways.

Sick Sibyl

The ecstasy that drives salmon upstream
to spawn and die, eels across oceans,
seal to their breeding grounds, deer hundreds
of miles north with the wolves who follow
to pick them off, geese winging south,
insects into fatal nuptial
flight – all united by
the spasm that verifies existence:
the ecstasy I never once
have felt – my ecstasy entirely
different, my ecstasy
a self-consuming sickness, an envy
of my questioners, who are one
with everything that lives and feels:
sustained, embraced, and blinded by
the shimmering haze which only my
sick eyes can pierce to see the truth,
the future, and the end of love.

Blocked Sibyl

Sullen and stubborn, self willed,
stupid, or just plain finished
as a sibyl – sometimes it happens
that way: one day, someone
who'd seemed absolutely right
for the job will dry up.
Hair messed, skin blotched, eyes
angrily or hopelessly
averted (but it's easy to tell
she's been crying), she won't answer
even the simple question:
What is it? from her apprentice-attendants,
much less pronounce. Maybe
she's sickened by laurel-leaves, smoke
from the brazier, the sweet, foul stench
of anxiety. Better
be blind than always forced
to see those supplicating gestures.
Secretly, they've begun
to appall her – she's afraid that quite
soon she might break down,
laugh or weep with despair
at the most solemn moment. Finished
or freed: whichever, she knows
as well as they that she's useless
now, a blocked sibyl.

Rescue of the Sibyl

After our climb to that distant mountain plateau,
when at last we stood close to the chasm's dangerous
   edge,
and leaned across the shaky wooden railing
to fathom what lay hidden in its depths,
from that opening rose a smell as harsh as ashes
dowsed with water, a curling vapour dank
and raw as floats above a marshy waste.

An aged creature, her guardian, perhaps,
uncocked his rifle, began his tired patter.
'Those steps lead down to the quaking rocks. In the
   deepest
cave, our famous sibyl sits on her tripod,
chewing laurel leaves and prophesying.
I am the only one who can interpret
every word she speaks. For a fiver I'll take the lot.'

But we gave him money to go away instead,
and the other two unpacked their sensible macs
and brandy flasks for protection against the damp.
How thoughtless and deprived I felt, as well
as freezing cold. I hadn't prepared myself
at all for the expedition, hadn't even
formulated one serious question.

The sides of the cleft were slick and wet, they curved
away like vertigo. As though peering through torn
drifting cloud from a plane when a current of air clears
   the curdled

atmosphere, I saw something moving, a horrible
dancing, the stones were revolving, atoms of earth
vibrating and boiling. There were groans and flashes of
   lightning.
Then the fumes blew back, thicker than before.

The bravest among us moved toward the abyss.
With each rung trod, the turbulence retreated.
She drove it below – a sullen, defeated dragon.
The staircase lay exposed as a flimsy construction,
and there on the mud and grit at the bottom, stood
   smudge-pots
and clumsy machines to delude any watchers, convince
them the rocks had been quaking. Ashamed, we
   followed her steps.

That poor wretch, the oracle, terrorized and abused,
stammered and rolled back her eyes when we finally
   found her.
It was months since she'd seen daylight or breathed fresh
   air.
Between her teeth were half-chewed laurel leaves, and
   her mouth
and chin were stained from their juice. Anxious and
   trembling,
like a hostage newly released from her ordeal,
she could not believe that rescue had come through a
   dream.

The Persian Sibyl

The Persian sibyl should be approached at dusk.
Revelation does not prosper in clear light.
She turns her book and face away to the shadows,
retreats into the core of the cloud of unknowing –
prefers to guess what is written there, that ageing
gentle witch, and that you do not see her expression
Mysteries only disclose their presence
to one who is cursed with the power of apocalypse.

The Sibyls in Amiens Cathedral

Thin-waisted Gothic sibyls
with pale calm faces
under wimples of clean Flanders linen,
holding your classical
attributes in elegant
fingers: the book,
the palm, the sword, the scroll;
images eaten
away and fading back
into the flaking
painted plaster and stone.

I can just distinguish which
is the Delphic one,
the Libyan, the Cumaean;
though your look and style
are those of later days,
Christian times;
your colours the gold and blue
of chapel banners,
soft madder pinks and reds
of hawthorn flowers,
lush Somme-river green.

Your sister, the Tiburtine,
told Augustus
of Christ's coming, and so,
as oracles
of his triumph, on these cathedral
walls you stand

with the Prophets – proud pagan women,
half-forgotten:
like the message you brought once,
but long ago,
to troubled northern souls.

The Sibila

*sung at midnight on Christmas Eve by a young boy
dressed in a rich, long robe and carrying a sword,
in the Church of San Bartolomé and Nuestra Señora
de Bonany, co-patrons of Soller de Mallorca,
Islas Baleares.*

The Day of Judgement comes
when there will be no Holy Service.
The Universal King of man,
God Eternal, then will judge us –
to everyone deliver justice.

Terrible fires will tear Heaven apart.
Lakes, springs, and rivers all aflame.
Even the fish will scream.

To the good He will say,
Come my blessed children
possess the Kingdom
which has been waiting
since the world was first created.

Humble Virgin, who this night gave birth
to infant Jesus, pray
He guard us from damnation's wrath.

With great severity and sternness
to the wicked He will say,
Go, evil ones, to everlasting torment
to the fire eternal,
to the Inferno and your Prince of Darkness.

The Libyan Sibyl

She casts away her clothes like soul's ascent
from the world of matter, shining arms upraised;

appears about to move with the ease of a dancer:
a hind setting its feet on the highest place.

Blinded by heavenly light, her eyes are closed.
What need of text – her message a psalm of praise?

It has come, the triumph of love above understanding:
ardour and ecstasy and eternal grace.

The Phrygian Sibyl

Speaking the language the first humans spoke
on that mountain plateau, homeland of Kybele,
Great Mother of the Gods, goddess
of caverns and wild beasts – words
only her eunuch-priests now
can understand – always, at the beginning
of spring, when the frenzy of lamentation
and blood-letting has changed to joy at His
rebirth, the Phrygian sibyl, possessed,
blesses the whole earth – rivers,
herds of horses, flowering vines
and lovers – making the oldest promise:
eternal life in the name of the Mother.

The Shinto Sibyl

White snow settles on the sacred peak,
white clouds drift between the cedar boughs,
white bear and antelope, wild boar, run there.
White boulders mark the ever-trodden path.
White the robes the ancient pilgrims wear.
White the sunrise through the eastern door.

Long white hair hung down the sibyl's back,
white flowers from the branches of her crown.
White light reflected by her flashing glass,
white papers fluttered on the stick she bore.
White stone the pavement where the miko* danced,
white drum she beat, and white her moving feet.
White sound I could not understand, her song.
Dead-white, but open-eyed, her face in trance.
White eagle-feathers left upon the shrine.
White bird that cried her message to me: 'Pure.'

* priestess, sibyl

The Tiburtine Sibyl

Albunea, nymph and sibyl of Tibur,
from your temple grove above the river's gorge
always you see the world through the spectral mist
of those plunging falls. The plain below spreads wide
and further west, upstream, like Hera's milk,
white water rises from a primal source.
Entering, at first, in spite of its warmth,
you shudder – then, the sulphur bites, tormenting
as the centaur's poisoned shirt. With head
rolled back and sunken eyes, you prophesy:
and all the richest senators of Rome,
the emperor himself, accept each word
of warning and advice as sent by Hercules,
the god they worship here – whose voice comes forced
and husky from your throat as his was when
he climbed onto the funeral pyre; whose holy
rites you celebrate with mystery,
wild-olive fires, and serpent sacrifice:
his priestess, oracle, and virgin-bride.

The Oracle at Dodona

The oak is full of doves, they nest in clefts
among its naked boughs. This oak
is the oldest tree in the world. Homer wrote of it.
Here, Zeus rules with Dione, child
and sister of Uranus (though some say,
instead, of her brother Oceanus), prophesies
through the throats of doves, doves they call oracles.
Three Doves – three women cloaked in furs,
with calloused unwashed feet, who must never
   break connection of their flesh from mother-
earth. Doves' voices speak gods' words. The women
stretch their vowels to sound like doves burbling.

Suddenly, the doves' murmuring
is drowned by the clangour of bronze rousing
the sanctuary – chains of a scourge in the hand
of a bronze statue, which every gust of wind
makes clash against a hollow gong and echo.
Someone has come to have his fate confirmed.
The stylos bit into the soft lead strip
as he wrote the question. The doves approached. They
   stamped
their feet on the muddy grass. The doves in the trees,
the circling reverberation of bronze, their song,
and the oak-wood lots in the black, snake-painted jar,
agreed. 'Yes.' All would be as he wished.

A Young Sibyl

At first she appears
candid and chaste,
yet when she stands
in front of the altar, opens
her mouth, and the voices start
to speak through her throat
in that plangent blare,
everything is changed.
Does she draw down the power
or does the god ride her?

The sanctuary is dark
but her slender form
grows larger, seems
surrounded by a glare,
a holy nimbus.
The odour of stables
is stronger than incense,
and blurring all her phrases –
the snapping of reins
and champing of horses.

Ageless, sacred mare
who gallops unshod –
one of Apollo's steeds –
over past and future.
Those words have meant war.
Blameless though dangerous,
her gnomic sentences
bring secrets back to light,
unriddle old mysteries
and knot new ones.

Introspection of a Sibyl

If only I could be aware of what is happening
in that void, that gap, that murky, fathomless cleft
where space and time must exist
between inspiration and the sound of my own voice:
the truth I never once have heard
a moment earlier than my listeners.

But I am no more conscious of the prophesies
than I can understand the language of birds.
A bird is singing now.
In spite of legend, like everyone else,
I wonder and guess at its message.
My oracles come like bird-song – or how I imagine
they must begin to sing – by instinct:
neither needing nor able to think.

The most terrible phrases burst from my mouth.
My profession is to doom strangers.
Already, as a girl,
playing ball with my friends in the village square
or feeding my tame pigeon, I remember
being even more appalled than my parents
by what I'd say: an unforgiveable insult
dealt out in all innocence, or a blurted sentence
like a gift to confirm good fortune.

How I admire control, and yearn to achieve it.
I've become almost grateful to those who control me.
Before, I never knew when it would begin,
the demon or angel invade me;

realized by the closed, startled expressions
on the faces of those standing round
– as though shutters crashed down –
that again I'd defined or foretold,
unerringly exposed the poor secret
some old man kept hidden all his life:

with sight as sharp as an eagle
who spots the single darting creature
veering back and forth, exhausted,
on a barren rocky mountainside,
maddened by the shadow of its wings –
and heavier than every element,
surer than the laws of gravity,
swoops for the kill.

After a few times, you recognize
a universal wariness. It takes longer
to fear yourself, to accept the certainty
of never illuminating that blankness –
that vital hiatus when the demon or angel,
the god, perhaps, takes possession
and you don't exist
yet have the power of a god.

Panic of falling – said to be
the sole inborn fear of a human infant.
Deeper than fear, I've learned, lies the greatest pleasure:
nausea and exhilaration of plummetting free –
the glee of surrender to nullity,

temptation more primal than any craving
for security: watching
the slow retreat of the gods, their stronghold
in flames, withdrawing from toppling towers,
abandoning our earth forever.

And the price for such knowledge? To have
absolutely no command over your life,
your words – no possibility
of calculated effects or tactics or policy.
But how useful you can be to others; and how lucky
if rather than burning or stoning, they protect you,
feed you, and let the simple folk praise you,
keep you safe as a caged bird –
and call you a sibyl.

Others

Only the Magpie

Only the magpie among all its kind
had to be caught for the Ark, and ever since
bear Noah's curse. Yet, beyond thought, more
acute than any thought, his rush of pale
and dark against the clouds and shooting twigs
evoke that time before the Fall when just
the wish to fly created wings and skill.

In paradise, fulfilment and desire
were close as white to yolk of an egg – rapture
continuous. Now, desire destroyed
by its pursuit, the bird of joy cannot
evade the hunter's net. Meanwhile, out
on the lawn, harsh chatter of magpies who pose
sidle and hop, pull worms, lift off, and never
wonder which pinion to use first.

Time's Metaphors

Four paw-marks filled with frozen water,
white brush-strokes drawn on a dark kimono
clutched against her haunches, bird-claw
hieroglyphs; the last surviving
haws and this spring's thrusting buds
enclosed by ice on the same frail twig.

Danger Areas

The landscape, hazed, recedes in layers,
pale heifers munching in the meadows,
hills crowned with castles as in fairy-tales.

Those little touches so essential
to create the state of tension
that brings the picture into focus.

It must be strange. Deceptive comforts
of familiarity are not
effectual, are not allowed.

Otherwise, why does he seek
the dragon; why is she, so languid
at the window, hoping for catastrophe.

Romance, that necessary irritant,
becomes the only explanation
of sojourn in such danger areas.

Driving Northward

There are stretches of road I remember,
autumn mist moving across a meadow,
driving northward, going home for the winter.

Such landscape is never spectacular.
A moment between dark trees and a river,
an outside curve, stones marking its contour,

and glowing with sunset, a segment
of the circling, luminous heavens.
Places where the mystery and terror

of the unavoidable future,
in spite of summer plans, reveals itself
certain only to be unexpected

as, beneath the wheels, that darting creature,
our panic swerving; whatever lies ahead
around the coming corner.

The Route Napoleon

Pollarded trees produce new growth –
this year's twigs and leaves displayed
as evidence. Trees marked by cryptic
streaks of paint, posters, reflector-disks
pressed into their trunks, wounds roughly dressed
with tar. Trees planted to absorb
the fumes of traffic, clothe embankments
and disguise the motorway.
Trees used; trees with the hopeless, doomed
servility of mutilated slaves
or trophy prisoners from some
forgotten war. Trees that can
no longer represent another realm
or further possibility,
but stand there, rooted, by the side
of the road, trapped as much as any
speeding driver or his passenger.

Trees

Trees, our mute companions,
looming through the winter mist
from the side of the road, lit for a moment
in passing by the car's headlamps:
ash and oak, chestnut and yew;
witnesses, huge mild
beings who suffer the consequence
of sharing our planet and cannot move
away from any evil we
subject them to, whose silent
absolution hides the scars of our sins,
who always forgive – yet still assume
the attributes of judges, not victims.

Deadheading the Roses

All day I clip the withered blossoms from the roses,
cut back till where at join of stem and leaf
I sense the chance of one more flower.

I work against maturity and the full cycle,
try to stop the dull hips from ripening
and using that energy

I want to divert towards more buds and flowers,
repeat the same glory, achieve what yet
I know to be impossible:

rejuvenated immortelles – far easier than
to accept the pressure of further growth,
the destiny that hardens petals

into firm, streaked knobs of seed disdaining beauty
for the sake of the future: that power
the artless rose-bush manifests.

Because every rose on the trellis witnesses how
nothing can halt the closing of one phase
or shorten the interval between

fruition and death. While I tear my hands on thorns
in a losing fight against autumn, the same
wind parching the roses' leaves

is driving me nearer to my destination. Only
some miracle could force new flowering,
another scented season.

The New Tree

Planted a tree the afternoon before
what has become the first evening of autumn
(eucalyptus-spring in Australia),
wind dropped and clouds moved on, mid-August storms
seemingly gone. And now the moon, almost
at full, a thin-worn disk of beaten tawny
metal foil, or crumpled papery fallen
eucalyptus leaf, hovers above the hawthorn
and the bramble hedges, unkempt corner
of my northern garden, as I cross the lawn
to touch the newly planted tree, its short
rose-madder stems and glaucous foliage, once more,
and wonder if its roots can feel the draw
of the antipodes, the pull from that far shore;
confirm again that everything's in order,
and wish it well until tomorrow's dawn.

Weeds

No matter what else happened that day,
if I weeded the garden, half-way to sleep,
I see only weeds and a close-up of earth,
muddy or crumbling like powder; red stems
of fat-hen, leathery thistles, ragwort
or nettles — as though the task released
responses scored into my brain,
inherent as my expectations.
For centuries, between tall rows
of corn and ripening beans, my people
must have stooped and hoed and dug,
repeating the same gestures, to root
those images so deeply, strongly.

The generations fall away.
Again I am the girl who worked hard
and gossipped with her village friends
about the weather and the boys,
the prospect of harvest. I can remember.
The weeds encroach. No matter what
may change, the crops are due that labour.
Though here and now, today (this chance
hiatus in reality
made by geography and money)
I weed my garden as a pleasure,
not forced by hunger. And yet the weeds
have their own power to nourish me.

Without Naomi

Gleaning the same ground over and over
the pickings get thinner.
From dusty earth and pallid short stubble,
dun flanks of this valley,
she cannot lift her eyes up to the hills.
Under the sky's low bowl
their shape hurts her, says better than words
that she is a stranger,
an alien, come from the wilderness
to serve as a witness
for the anguish and stigma of learning
to love what does not nourish.
Exile feeds on memory, but her country
has no history. She
only remembers legends and dreams.
Until she finds the courage
to claim it, her heritage will never
be more than this bare field.

She gleaned the same ground over and over.
Each seed recovered
she planted and watered, moved every stone
that might stifle its growth;
to keep it warm at night through the winter
in the open field she slept.
Hills that once seemed hostile changed their aspect,
now provided shelter
from bitter cold and snow and shrivelling wind.
When spring came, it flourished,
her corner of the acre: secret garden,
green-tasselled wheat-child –
consolation and hope for the future.
She worked with the others
when the time came for harvest. They taught her
their songs and language, smiled
and spoke of a marriage, grain to be milled;
bread, not dreams, as birthright.

New Year in England

Red tiles on the huddled village roofs
fusing into the smoky glow,
the marshland and hills, the mist which makes
a floating crimson lake of light
the sun's last fanning rays illuminate,
the further arch of winter blue.
The clouds also demand their praise –
those purple banners, and corded nap
of new-ploughed earth. Yet something is lacking.

This calm afternoon
of early January, when all the world
still feels as if resting from festival,
needs more lauding, more
gratitude, than the empty road
and separate houses, heraldic television
aerials, the silhouetted
tower of the vacant church,
seem able to express. And I
wait hopeful and uncertain if
fit words will come: the glory-song
to satisfy such daunting trust.

The First of October

At the turn of the seasons
that feeling –
         mournful
uneasy   uncertain
leaves falling in autumn, days shortening,
or in spring, chill watery sunlight,
blurred colours emerging
as rain washes away the husk
of the whole winter's grime
from tree-trunks and buildings
– when the spirit is naked and cringing.
It's the same in October.
Rain also is working the changes
stripping the trees
mulching leaves into the gutter.
But sometimes
         washing off mud
brings back a flash of summer's tones:
a leaf plaqued
against the pavement, clear
amber yellow and topaz brown.
The equinox.
Earth at midway point.
Any movement now
must take us further out
or closer to the sun.
When the planet balances
perhaps it needs
and draws upon
even my equilibrium.

The Daisy Chain

Susan with a daisy chain.
A young girl waiting. She wants
to make it long enough
to span the world.
Musing between two states:
ignorance and innocence
boldness and fear
essentially entwined.
She winds the chain
around her neck
holds out the other end
as if to offer it
her maiden gift
and wanders towards the field.

Susan in the field
looking for her bull to deck.
She wants to crown that space
of curling hair between
the horns. She binds
the flower chain
around his head
and strokes his rufous flanks
admires the lashes
of his enormous eyes.
His back is broad and wide
his shoulders powerful
his legs as fine
as heroes' in her dreams.

Susan beneath the trees.
He tossed his head
and tore the daisy chain.
In spite of what she dreamed
her gentle bull
was not a unicorn.
She comes back home to sit
cross-legged on the lawn
and make another chain
to decorate herself
sing songs and plait
the daisies in her hair
to while away the time until
her waiting ends.

With David in the Nimrud Galleries

His first words, after we passed under
the archway into the rooms of the Nimrud reliefs,
were to question why the crabs, claws uplifted
heraldically between fish and floating horses
with soldiers' corpses tangled in their reins,
incised on the golden limestone tablets, were shown
eight-legged. Further in, we rode behind
Ashurbanipal to the lion-garden,
where the beasts were released from their cages to be shot
(a rich man's safari); then followed with his men
to Marduk's temple to make the sacrifice.
He noted how delicately the shallow streams
of blood from the arrow-wounds had been graved down
 the lions'
sides, like the river's waves; and pointed out
a gazelle turning to reassure her fawn,
and two birds fluttering above a palm.

This precise observation confirmed my pleasure, and his.
I wondered about the craftsmen who did these carvings.
The columns of captives are endless: how they bind
the composition together. Such strong horizontals:
women, children. One too small to walk
into slavery straddles his father's shoulders.
On another tablet a group of prisoners have
abased themselves. So many battles: Thebes,
Tyre, the Elamite cities. Cunning use
of diagonals: lances, slanting siege ladders.
So many exiles. Centuries later these
black streaks across a sinewy leg

or fierce helmetted head pitted and stained
by rain and erosion are the only signs left by nomads
who built their meagre fires and sheltered among
ghosts and jackals sharing the ruins of Nimrud.

All Assyria to be imagined
from these fragments. After millennia
of neglect, now they are treated as carefully
as premature babies. Every showcase of weapons,
vases, or jewellery with its own humidity
and temperature recorder. We could hear
the humming of machinery, concealed
neon-lighting and air-conditioning. Alone
in the gallery as scribes in a library,
I try to tell him what I remember: a wordy
confusion of Bible tales and Mongol invasions,
time's desolations. Politely he ignores
the disturbance, clearly more absorbed and delighted
by friezes of lions, muscled priests with taloned
feet and the heads of vultures, banquets and triumphs:
this precious detritus of Nimrud before his eyes.

Childhood

I see it like an illustration in a magazine:
the low and seemly blocks of middle-class apartment
   buildings,
with half-grown trees and sprinkled lawn between;
   colours neither
pale nor garish but chosen from the clear, most popular
and tasteful range: grass-green, sky-blue, an
   undemanding red, and
pointillistic touches from parked cars, fire-hydrants,
   freshly-varnished
doors and window-frames. The streets do not run
   straight: the land
is hummocky, its dips and curves are on a human scale.

Here on the hill-crest where I stop to contemplate my
   whole
domain, I feel as powerful and joyful as the wind
that forms the clouds each moment into different shapes.
I wonder at the lives of such exemplary inhabitants,
confirm again that everything's in order, just as it should
   be
in Toytown; and only then I nod my head and check the
   straps
and buckles of my skates, let myself go, and swoop
   down, down,
past houses, families, up the opposite slope and into
   Heaven.

The Message

Hard to remember how long ago it started –
blankets drawn close round my shoulders, or in summer only
a sheet – dragging whichever near enough
to my short-sighted gaze to see the glistening fibres
silhouetted against an open door or window,
any source of light to define them standing upright
or angled, in regular series like letters. Eyes smarting,
I would stare for hours at the wispy lines:
that mysterious script, that wizard's calligraphy.

Sometimes I could disentangle single
words (mostly my own name), but never
the whole sentence potential in the fabric's
weave and texture, shadowy, waiting; marked
already on the sheep's back, grown with the cotton's
flowering; survived through washing, carding, spinning
and dyeing – every process in the chain of hazard
before it reached me, safe in my room, protected
by the wallpaper's pattern: those trellised roses
whose awful thorns baffled discovery.

No matter how I tried, though my brain felt
like a sponge being squeezed by large indifferent hands
and my eyes unfocused, it never showed clear. Yet even
now, when I wake with the dawn, or at night when the
    crumpled
bedding is furrowed with lamplight, if I twist my head
or slide down the bed, the same letters appear, just
as unreadable, just as insistent to be read –
the message that will be decoded by no one but me.

A Child Crying

Gasps and sobs through the wall from the next flat:
a child's voice in dirge-like complaint whose words
I cannot make out but whose tone accords too well
with my mood – as though it were I in that stranger's
 room,
bitter and desolate, choked with grief,
oppressed by a world I cannot understand,
that withdraws and refuses to console me.

A child crying. We who can imagine
that to batter the child to silence would be
kinder than to leave it in such distress
(at least would change our own distress), each time
are forced back to that old anguish – hours shut into
a bedroom, crouched behind a slammed door,
stifling in a wardrobe, throbbing temples
pressed against a bathtub; trapped horror
of the cot, suffocating blankets, the sickly
baby colours of their damp itching.

And when at last it has stopped, and the unknown child
is pacified, we are left exhausted and
ashamed as though after torture, capitulation,
and the final loss.

Almost-Full Moon

First through one window,
then moving to the other,
she looks at me all evening,
sitting at my desk. But
I'm only one of the creatures
the almost-full moon watches.
There are so many rooms and houses,
so many open windows,
so much to see, such huge
responsibility.
She supervises moths,
moles, and hedgehogs; owls,
orchards, and empty beaches;
and wakeful, lonely children
who stare up at the face
of the calm white mother,
till soothed, their heads roll sideways
on the pillow, into shadow,
and they fall asleep.

That Smile

Sometimes I find myself looking at children
with that fond soft smile of older women
who've forgotten it all; which made me hate them
when I was yearning for confirmation
of my new maternal status, a decade ago.

But yesterday, though I should have known better
(in spite of those memories), shut into
a carriage on the Northern Line
with a distracted mother and her two small boys,
I felt that same expression blur my features.

Sturdy, rosy, laughing, bundled into anoraks,
pressing their noses flat against the windows,
the naughty children crawled across arm-rests,
gabbled utter nonsense and mixed-up words,
ignoring their mother's restraints and protests.

Truer to their humanity than either
of us, they knew without having to learn
that for the short time given – whether it was
going to end at Edgware or in seventy years –
the only purpose of living is pleasure.

Maybe the smile that used to disconcert
had a different meaning than I read into it.
Those other women might have been trying
to reassure and divert me, as I now
wanted to catch the mother's furious eye

and make her delight in them, acknowledge her ow
two children as emanations of wisdom
and joy; and more than this, as empty
station platforms hurtled past,
I wished that she would smile at me.

Domestical

When, instead of scrubbing their jeans, I'm washing
my own clothes, it doesn't feel like doing housework –
my labours neither justified nor sanctified –
no one I can blame or accuse

When I open a box of matches and see one
is broken or shorter, or has a half-formed head,
it's that one I choose

The tainted grapes on the bunch: those with a spot
of mould, softening away from the stem, I pick
and eat first – and the squashed tomato, blackening
banana, the pork-chop without any kidney

Whatever is perfect, or beautiful, or new,
I carefully save for a special occasion –
my wardrobe full of unworn, old-fashioned shoes

And the smile on my face is like make-up over a wound
or a birthmark, to hide my resentment and envy:
calm of the over-cautious

But because I have always been waiting (augmenting
impatience), I sense how the others avoid me,
fearing a breakdown, potential of chaos,
genie let loose from the bottle

Because I will not admit what I think, I have
no opinions; never admit what I want,
have forgotten my needs; never admit who I am,
have lost my name and freedom

Until this huge discomfort constitutes
my whole existence – called to act a part
for which I'm completely unsuitable.

It Must

Friends, sisters, are you used to your face in the mirror?
Can you accept or even recognize it?
Don't be angry, answer me frankly, excuse
the question's crudity. I can't – no matter
how often I take the little square of glass
from my bag, or furtively glance into shop-windows,
the face reflected back is always a shock.

Those scars and wrinkles, the clumping of pigment
into moles, spots, faulty warty growths
around hairline and neck, the way skin's texture changes
absolutely, becomes roughened and scaly,
coarse-grained, every pore visible, as though
the magnification were intensified: horrible.
These days, I prefer firmer flesh in close-up.

Younger, I remember how I stared, with a mixture
of attraction, repulsion, and pity, at the cheeks of older
women – the sort I chose for friends. Did they
need me as much as I idealized them?
There seemed something splendid and brave about such
    raddled
features, crusted and blurred with the same heavy
    make-up
I've taken to wearing – warpaint, if, as they say,
the real function of warpaint is to bolster
the uncertain warrior's spirit, more than to
undermine and terrify his opponent.

Now, I long to ask my friends these very
questions and compare reactions, blurt out
the taboo words. But we're so polite, so lavish
with compliments, tender, protective – cherishing
the common hurt: tenderness of bruised flesh,
darkness under the eyes from held-back tears,
watery blisters on frost-touched fruit already
decaying, marked by death's irregularities.

Friends, tell me the truth. Do you also
sometimes feel a sudden jaunty indifference,
or even better, extraordinary moments
when you positively welcome the new
face that greets you from the mirror like
a mother – not your own mother, but that other
dream-figure of she-you-always-yearned-for.
Your face, if you try, can become hers. It must.

Anja's Poem

A friend told me
to keep all combings –
the loosened hairs
that fell into my lap,
onto my shoulders,
after shampooing –
and save them till I'm old
to flatter and augment
my thinning tresses.

I liked the thought.
It has become
a weekly usage,
almost my only form
of piety.
As I gather
the clean hairs, twist them
around my fingers, and
put them in the special
box behind the mirror
in a corner
of my dressing table,
I feel connected to
a host of women, ageing
or youthful, present, past
and future; part of a
continuity, that
basic history
indifferent

to boundaries, unmoved
by proclamations.

Like them, though old, I'll want
to look the best I can;
not to compete, or prove
I still can be a beauty,
but out of pride
and my own dignity,
in honour of
my family and
the peaceful, fruitful land.

And when I'm dead, I hope
my hair will be arranged
by careful women's hands
in memory of
its onetime glory;
that round my head they'll loop
the heavy rope
of all the hair I'll have
lived long enough to save,
as if a crown,
for my best ornament,
before they fold the cloth
over my face.

Divination by Hair

1
Every few days, looking into the mirror,
I find another dozen hairs turned white.
Though dubious about my purpose, almost
despising myself, I go on pulling them out.
She, the ideal I stubbornly adhere to,
would never search so urgently for their wiry
glint, crane her neck awkwardly
the better to ensure not one escapes
the tweezer; she would disdain pursuit of such
discoveries. White hairs are curlier
and vigorous, age and death becoming
more assertive the closer they approach.

I know it can be nothing but a losing
battle, paltry and ridiculous.
Sooner or later I'll have to choose whether
to be bald or white. I cannot continue
this depilation with impunity.
They'll never grow back as fast as vanity
can raze them. As if enthralled (it cannot
be mere scrutiny distorts my face)
hours at a time I stand in front of my mirror,
which long before now should have lost its power
and become a superseded altar, not
the secret place of panic, rage, and grief.

I'd prefer to be brave, to let my tresses fade
to mottled grey and white – but even the best
resolutions are hard to keep when every
day's attrition brings a new defeat.

If only it could happen overnight:
one morning I would wake transformed into
that dignified wise matron of my dreams,
matured at last to grace – though I make her sound
like the grandmother on a birthday card,
not at all what I mean (how to convey
the essence of a person realized?) –
storms calmed, reefs passed, safe harbour now in sight.

2
Every day, new hairs faded.
Why don't I just accept it?
Why don't I dye it? What difference
would it make if I left them? Age
would not come sooner, nor my actions
avert dissolution and death.
Who do I think I'm fooling?
– No one except myself.
For who cares really whether
my hair is grey, white, or black?
Like others, I try my best
to conceal, refuse, forget.

3
Because death always seemed a mother –
or a grandmother – someone
familiar, now I come near
the time of greying hair, I fear
the mask more than the skull beneath.

4
Silver hair is the warning sign.
To watch it spread is like catching fire.
I want to smother it, to hide
the mark that shows I'm next in line,
exposed, too near the danger-zone.
I feel death creeping up behind.
Those fading hairs and deepening lines
are the entangling net she throws.

5
Witch from an ancient forest-tale;
goddess; hag; Atropos-Fate;
Kali; crone. Can I placate
you better by carefully hiding the blaze
you sear across my brow, or apeing
your style? Conquering queen, your embrace
is inexorable. Whether I hate
or deny or adore you, you will unmake
me, eternally, and create me again.

6
         days   mirror
          dozen hairs   white
    dubious   purpose
despising
      ideal   stubbornly adhere
                urgently
                awkwardly
             not one escapes
                     pursuit

discoveries
    vigorous   age and death
   assertive   approach

                                 losing
battle   paltry   ridiculous
                            choose
     bald or white
             impunity
                        vanity
            enthralled
   scrutiny distorts
                    my mirror
                    lost its power
     a superseded altar
        panic, rage, and grief

          brave   tresses
  mottled grey and white   best
resolutions
    attrition   defeat
           overnight
          transformed
  dignified   dreams
        grace
    grandmother
        how   convey
 essence
   calmed   passed   harbour   in sight

Wisdom of the Mothers

That ugly rage
that snarl of hate which says
I made myself succumb
I played myself false
I suffered
so let it be the same –
   the shame
   the sense of loss
   the only pleasure left
   vindictiveness –
for all the others:
wisdom of the mothers.

Satellite

Light streams into the room:
a presence behind the curtains
pushing against their edges
as palpable
and menacing and volatile as mercury.
Suspended in an empty sky,
above the black back-drop of pines,
that scalding glare —
flattening the lawn into a bald formality.
How could I forget the full moon?

Only this afternoon
impossible to stop the tears
forced from my eyes and down my face:
a water-mask.
It's not a metaphor or an analogy.
Again and again I'm dragged off-course.
For days I could not wake — tonight,
quite lunatic,
I cannot sleep, but want to go outside, into
that light, and shriek at the moon.

I hope it will end soon.
And yet, if I withdraw beyond
her rule, through cowardice, or
she no longer
focuses her power and ceases to disturb,
how foiled and desolate I'll be:

a barren victory, gained
by banishment
from that world of extremity in which I've lived
as satellite to the moon.

Meeting

It would need witchcraft to see your face
of twenty years ago, and mine, revived,
confronted as if resurrected ghosts –

a banshee ceremony, screams and cries,
to call them back, those masks of flesh dissolved,
remade, and formed not by the grave but life.

What would the younger pair think of us now?
Might that half-wild girl still fall in love,
or you be charmed by what I have become?

Could who we were agree to such a future –
already our past, denied or mostly forgotten –
having our memories as foreknowledge?

How can there be a hope of recognition
when every cell has been renewed and altered,
the pattern coarsened through repetition?

Yet those four, meeting like strangers
outside time and matter's flux, accept
their actuality, and never question

the others' realness. Amazed and fascinated,
they wait to hear confirming words, or intercept
the one appropriate gesture of release.

Again

Suppose the prince who once had been a toad
changed back after a certain span of years.
Perhaps it always was intended.
Happily ever after only meant
a few decades, and this return to earlier
days inexorably programmed into
the experiment. The kindly fairy's
blessing lost its potency as princess
and her golden hero aged together.

Suppose one morning when he woke he felt
the clammy stricture web his toes and fingers,
his mouth begin to stretch into that
recollected lipless grin; and when she turned
to face him from her pillow, saw in her
contracting pupils the reflection of
cold warts and freckles surfacing like blisters
on his muddy skin. He dared not speak,
but waited, numb with hopelessness and dread.

Suppose that night she'd dreamed about the hour
her ball had rolled and splashed into the pool
and that foul toad had hopped towards her, croaked
his arrogant demand, and forced her will.
Yet afterwards, everything was perfect.
As though the time between had vanished, now
she smiled and clung to him, gazed deep into
unaltered eyes. Who could guess the coming
transformation? Let it all begin again.

Animal Tamer

You would have made a good animal tamer –
I can tell by the way you're taming the wild black cat
that appeared last week at the bottom of the garden.
Every morning she comes a little further.
You go outside with a half-filled saucer of milk
and put it down as if you didn't care,
but each day move it an inch nearer the door.

The black cat's glaring eyes have a baffled look.
There's something about you she cannot understand.
You've activated her curiosity.
But still she crouches watchful under the bushes
until you glance away and fuss with your pipe,
and then she dashes across and gulps and laps,
the hair round her neck bristling with suspicion,
peering up at you several times a minute,
relieved and yet puzzled by such indifference,
as though she missed the thrill of flight and escape.

Today, for the very first time, you turned and stared
at those yellow, survivor's eyes, and the cat stared back
a moment before she swerved and ran to safety.
But then she stopped, and doubled round and half
gave in, and soon, as I know well, you'll have
that cat, body pressed down on the earth and fur
electrified, stretching her limbs for mercy.

Any Old Couple

Young and arrogant, I thought romantic love
was rare, a pleasure only few might know.
That old couple, parents or strangers,
surely they never had borne what made my life
a privileged torment? Taboo-masks, frightening or
ridiculous, their visages seemed, fabulously
netted with lines and patches of darkening pigment.
Impossible they could have swooned like us.

But now in my turn I'm becoming one of the elders,
I see the same implacable conviction
reflected from bright, impervious, almond-shaped eyes
set cleanly in smooth sockets barely impressed
above glowing curves of flesh. While remembering
when someone my present age seemed an ancient, I'm
    aware
that soon I'll be merely another out-of-date monster
they can scoff at and politely disbelieve.

How time has changed my view of any old couple
smiling together, no longer finding it
necessary to insist. I've been finally
humbled by the knowledge that, yes, they also
felt it, the ordinary human lot, every
ecstasy I suffered, the same pain and glory
the children are just beginning to enjoy,
which we all share perhaps until death.

Going Back

There was only a six-year gap
between leaving and going back
yet they all looked like amateur actors.

Under eyebrows grown thicker –
surely they'd not been so wrinkled? –
eyes darted like confidence tricksters.

Clumsy, those lines on their faces.
And someone inexpert had shaken
talc over their heads. The make-up

was awful, but worse, their attempts
and behaviour as elders: gestures
compounded of pomp and burlesque.

They were children aping grown-ups:
subdued husband, bustling
wife, utter failure or success.

The first unguarded shock,
pity and horror,
forced to stare into that mirror

when we met, after only six years.
But in less than an hour, all such fears
were blurred by laughter's easy tears.

The Function of Tears

The function of tears
must be to serve as language,
a message to others –
yet the bitterest weeping
takes place alone. The message
then for oneself, an urgent
attempt to reach
that shackled prisoner
in the deepest dungeon
far below the level
of the lake.

What do tears express
that words cannot do better?
Tears are the first language –
a glazed face and anguished
moans communicate
rage, pride, regret;
pleasure or frustration;
remorse and hatred:
almost every emotion
sufficiently intense,
before words can be formed.

Each of these feelings
in turn must colour
the soul of the prisoner
abandoned in her corner,
like the shifting greys
tinged by rainbow hues

of light filtered
through tears clogging
her lashes, jagged
prisms of memory
and hope in the gloom.

Such tears have little effect
on the silent warder
who checks the links
of her chain, brings bread
and drinking water
and sometimes even
changes the musty straw.
No one has ever seen
the warder cry —
not his wife or children,
not the torturer.

Perhaps the lake
was hollowed out by tears.
But until the castle
is assailed, beseiged,
completely undermined —
with dungeons flooded,
crenellations tumbling —
and torturer, warder,
and prisoner are forced
to shout above the sound
of rushing water,

call to each other for rescue,
swim clear of the ruins,
embrace and cry with relief –
that lake, like the socket
of a giant eye drowned
by unimaginable
grief, will still stare
blindly up toward heaven
and go on weeping,
endlessly replenished
from a fountain of tears.

Suddenly

suddenly the mail stops
the car won't start
the telephone stays silent

and *suddenly* becomes
an indeterminate phase
with no foreseeable limit

someone suddenly dies
there's still a part of life
ahead for those left

to learn how to survive
until this stasis ends
suddenly more time

Grief

As poison may produce its antidote
even grief be assuaged by itself
(as every hope fades) even grief abates.

That autonomic consequence,
its chemical results, which made
nerves wince, skin pale and flinch, brought sudden

sleep and agitated dreams,
oscillation through extremes,
a drench of tears unwilled as winter rain,

reaches saturation point.
The antidote, self-manufactured,
is elegant evidence of that fine system

of checks and balances which holds you
in the land of the living, impotent
as some laboratory monkey.

The purpose of the demonstration
proved: you don't succumb – immune
henceforth to this particular poison.

Not Well-Mapped as Heaven

I know so many people who are dead.
The thought always insists on coming in
the present tense. How often they return,
old friends, when I am half-asleep, or seated
at my desk. Mostly their state was changed
by suicide or heart-attack; rare,
the lingering deaths. And yet, like friends in life,
we drift apart. I move into the ageing,
they are spared. They won't grow old with me –
but that assertion doesn't mean I can
persuade myself to the belief that afterwards
those timeless dead and I will meet again.
Nevertheless, that place they are, surely
has more expanse and depth than merely my own
memory, though not well-mapped as Heaven.

The Thorn

Is the thorn blunted, or the heart scar-hardened
and calloused?
                    Only the grating fall
of earth thrown from a spade, loosened
from the new-dug clay and knocking
against the wooden lid as if
I heard it from inside, can alert
and alarm, can awake –
                         as though it needs
almost the trump of doom to make
me see: frost-locked, soot-rinded tree
growing near the cemetery
wall, and, balancing
sure-footed on its shaking branch,
that bird's wind-ruffled plumage; to make
me realize their hardihood
and valour.   The bird's breast pressed upon
the thorn obeys the laws of life
and bleeds, the bird must sing its song
of faith and praise; and when spring comes,
even this thorn-tree will be capped with
flowers above the healing grave.

My Rings

On my right hand since then
I've always worn the ring
my father and I chose
as my twenty-first birthday present.
On my left, these months
since her death, my mother's ring –
the engagement ring he bought her
half a century ago,
and gave to me,
after the funeral.

The only break in his grief,
those first mourning days,
was when he learned
the two of them would lie
together under the same slab.
Ten weeks later, throttled
to death by a cancer, he followed.

If I forget . . . then let
the faded garnet oval
in its antique setting
tighten round that finger
like a garotte; the diamond,
angular, stab sharp
up my arm and pierce my heart.

I spread my hands on the desk.
Prominent tendons and veins
on the back, like hers;

red worn skin of the palm
that chaps and breaks
so easily, inherited
from my father. Even without
the rings, the flesh of my hands
is their memorial.
No need for anything
more formal – not gold
nor platinum and precious stones
can serve as well
as these two orphaned hands.

Questions

How go on being angry with the dead,
remembering his mortuary face –
the chill when you bent and pressed your lips against
a substance no longer flesh: too cold, too dense;
the urge to take his body in your arms,
stretch out by his side: not believing any embrace
could warm him back to life, but simply a need
to lie with him there in the casket as though that
were your duty and pleasure. You wanted nothing else.

How go on being angry with the dead
when those last weeks of pain play themselves through,
over and over again – those sounds, those gestures.

The view from that room: luminous winter days.
The structure of a tree lit from every
angle. The setting sun sinking into
its cage of branches. After his death you lay down
on the bed to see exactly what he'd seen:
a glowing, endless sky, flushed and tender.

Yet unaffected by these memories,
still that anger. Is it only anger
because he died – the rankling of guilt you share
with everyone alive toward their dead,
a ruse of the brain to survive the time of grief;
or is it a true and valid anger against
the ones who brought you into the world to die
but taught you nothing about how to die,
and leave you now, weakened, the questions obscured.

Not Grief but Fear

It was less grief than fear
as I stood on the plastic grass
at the edge of your grave.
Fear of the grave –
the way the edging stopped
and the sides plunged
deeper than any hole
I'd ever peered into,
glistened and darkened downwards:
conglomerate of stones
and roots and spiders' nests –
a section through the foundations.

Fear, of course, for myself:
horror of suffocation
like that which comes at night
when the blankets press, crushing
the bones of my feet,
and the sheet across my mouth clings
like a membrane. Back into
the earth, dream of the time
before birth. Mother, you were too light
to bear the weight of my need.
My fear, entombed
with you, must resurrect.

Less grief than fear.
Now everything I do
though it seems in memory of you
is done to ward off the truth
of that death you've gone into
alone. Both fear and grief.
For though you loved me well,
your smoky torch glows faint
and only shows me pebbles dimly
glinting up ahead,
reflections from the clay,
but not the way.

Commemorated

I went to see your grave the other day –
a simple tombstone, white and plain, nothing
there except your names and those two dates,
just weeks apart, telling when you died.

This browning wisp of bindweed on my desk
was growing round the base. A tender mauve
and green, it was the only decoration.
Flowers had been far from my thoughts. Since then,

I cannot say if time goes fast or slow,
as those who read your names will never know
when you were born or who you were or your
relation to each other, nor why your deaths
should be commemorated, but not your lives.

Too Late

Maybe it happens one night, driving
through an unknown suburb, the realization
that nothing is going to change, the time
will never come for explanation –

(those touching fantasies of shedding
your armour, final reconciliation,
and no further need for defences:
a childhood dream of smiles and embracing).

Till now, such hopes were what sustained.
But every crossroad and junction demand
an instant decision, with no one to praise
or help you find your way in the dark.

And stopping underneath a street-lamp
to consult the map again,
suddenly you're sure the meeting,
though so longed-for, will not take place.

That night, lost, then arriving too late,
you understood why the others
(and you'd have done the same), could not wait.
They were gone. Your turn now to start.

Time Come

Hearing, 'His time had come,' do you think:
somewhere up there, archaic reassuring
plaster gods are smiling down,
leaning across a velvet padded rail –
the bar of heaven? Maybe their paint
is flaking, but behind them, the wheels and ratchets
turn, that giant, ramshackle mechanism:
diagram of ascendancies, cusps
and influence, the great computer
we're all plugged into, every last one
of the billions (more living now than ever
have lived before); but the system can still
contain them, process the information
and spew out the numbers and codes of every
single one when his time has come.

Or, if that garish circus backcloth
were stripped down, and the black emptiness
of the endless space behind should be revealed –
satin sheen inside the devil's cloak
as the old gallant swirls it (if there were a devil);
a glassy void reflecting nothing
but your own image back, each time
further away and more and more ghostly;
that realm of accident where no gods punish,
supervise, or favour: a world
of isolated atomies,
insurance-agents calculating odds
against the chances of before and after –
would you panic and curse, or have you always
known the secret of the universe?

Terra Incognita

A day that makes me feel I've lived already
long enough – almost forever; with nothing
else especially to wait for; as though
I've had as much as anyone can have,
both good and bad: a day it would not even
matter if the coming few decades
(the most to hope for) were to be erased
from my allotted tally. Is this a fear
of what portends, or recognition of
a lucky fate?
            What chafed, the bonds' constraint,
was my support. I never realized
the cords I strained to break were safety nets.
Failure can change into success of sorts,
perhaps. My perseverence led to just
this place. I must admit the paradox.

And yet I'm left in an absence of faith
so absolute that any suppositious
future mocks the prospect of change: awareness
which moves far beyond the spiralling,
recurrent plunge into despair – a region
unexplored –
          nor, on this calm, soft,
perfect autumn day, lets me forget
winter's worst storms still have to be faced.

That Coming Mystery

The longer you stare into its depths, the further
the fire recedes, the wider it spreads. Those knots
of heat, whirling eddies of light where the final
drops of sap lay hidden, untouched till now,
flare up, explode, as though a galaxy
were being born. Like staring into the eye
of a storm, when clouds are as turbulent as waves
beneath a cliff. If you look for too long at one
of these things it seems to surround you, and perhaps
for a moment you'll have the luck to become part of it,
to lose your separateness in the heart of whichever
element – in a water-bead, a flame,
the moving air, or rock and earth. What you watch
with such attentiveness is the breaking and re-creation
of matter's forms: that coming mystery
you cannot witness happen to yourself,
but strain to understand and to accept
before you must experience.

Fire

Fire, like all servants, must be watched
continually. Fire, the best servant,
therefore the most dangerous. Every
servant dreams to usurp his master, outdo
his arrogance and pomp, his whims, his cruelty.
Servants would create a world
of absolute caprice, a whole universe
moved by the same murderous
totalitarian ferocity as fire
runs riot through tenements, incandescing
block after block of their pattern: a chart lit up
to demonstrate the saturation bombing
(those who plot it being fire's unwitting
servants). Once got loose, fire will eat
metal box-cars and girders, cement structures,
papery bark of eucalyptus trees,
household pets or humans: consume anything.
Because nothing is alien to fire, as the perfect servant
never shows surprise at his ruler's demands,
but will supply whatever asked for. Contained,
fire can work miracles, but
rampaging free, reduces even his own
hearth to ashy desolation – then creeps
back, surly, to sit weeping in the ruins.

All Those Victorian Paintings

All those Victorian paintings, with camels,
and that eerie lavender light, just
after sunset, were absolutely right.
Not only Holman Hunt – yet goats
still scatter across the landscape like scraps
of burnt paper, or move down a hillside as though
a column of ants was approaching – but the other,
forgotten, painters (technique respectful
and serious as they once were):
ladies, cheeks flushed under plaited straw hats,
skirts dusty, with campstool, umbrella, and easel,
whose pictures of palm-trees and Arabs now stand
face to the wall in attics, or hang
in vicarage bedrooms; their bachelor cousins
and brothers, convalescents or artistic
consuls – saw the Holy Land
with a camera's focused accuracy –
triumph of objectivity
over such believers' fervour.

Belief

It was trying not to wake up from a nightmare
of willed descent into the maelstrom,
or, shrunk to the size of an atom,
forcing my way through the shuttered
iris of a kaleidoscope
into a glistening darkness of feathers
and suffocation, to learn what lay
behind that wall.

It was clinging to the top of the highest dizzying slide,
unable to let go, or,
petrified at the open door
of an aircraft, parachute pack on my back,
ripcord unfelt between paralysed fingers,
the roaring of wind, like sound come through ether,
a fading call.

Somewhere down there, hazed mountains in the distance,
the leathery saint sits in his cave,
wrestling with demons. Every attempt
takes place in a context of order and calm.
Hardest of all to give up the cold
excitement of hallucination:
a sword above the abyss that does not
ascend or fall.

Evening and Dawn

Clouds like enormous beckoning hands, like seraphim –
fiery wheels of heads and wings revolving before the
 throne
of God and heralding its approach.

A tinge of bronze on clouds the shape of a crane flying,
 legs
streaming behind; full moon poised over its head like a
 crown
and Venus the jewel on its anklet.

Sky clear and pure as a fresco at evening and dawn.

Dewy nap of lawn and dense firmness of silhouetted
 trees;
borders sharp-drawn between absorbent blackness
and blanched reflecting surfaces.

The sea rolling in, countless small glintings and flashings
as the source of radiance elevates and alters the shadows
continually.

An intensifying stillness, no wind, diminution of sound.

Every moment new awakenings.

Yet the longer I gaze at the garden, the more its
 substances
waver and fade into misty darkness.

In the augmenting morning heat, the stones on the beach take on weight and solidity; each separate atom dancing the glory of light.

Summer Storm

Only for some moments
the sky goes dark as night-time:
rain fuming up like smoke
from the tiled roofs opposite.
Sunshine, lightning, and thunder-roar.

And cold air slides in, heavy,
across ledges of windows
there was no time to close:
a dense and chilly flood
that rises from the floor.

Already the storm is moving.
The separate drops
of water slowing in the gutter-
pipes drum their muffled
tattoo, after the downpour.

Midsummer Night

Midsummer night. Light never leaves the sky.
Dull as cooling coal, the hurt sun lingers.
Bituminous stones, their black surfaces
scratched with runes only spirits can read
rise out of the beaches: backs of whales seamed
by scars, or stars that mark the sky's old wounds –
evidence of violence, and its omen.
There are fires. From below the horizon flames
smudge the clouds with crimson reflections, bloody
the outline of dunes and boulders. Between
midnight and morning not one soul comes
to witness the sun lurch itself up
and begin its pained slow wheeling towards
the field of darkness, the opposite solstice.

Squirrel in Holland Park

An after-lunch walk: autumn's first flaccid fallen leaves.
Canopied trees which held off the raindrops and filtered
the light. Between trunks plaqued with moss the
   squirrels approached,
tails buoyant as brush-strokes, self-assured as spoiled
   children.

The most confident of them all was blind on one side,
orb dull, shrunken, and white as the boiled eye of a fish.
With the other black, darting, totally alert eye
it judged the exact distance to reach the proffered nut.

Coat and shoes shabby, finger and hair the same
   tarnished
chemical yellow as those tense paws the squirrel thrust
out, when the man who was feeding it, clucking his
   tongue
and murmuring endearments, noticed me standing there,

with a confused gesture he nodded yet winced away,
his grasp tightening over the crumpled paper bag.
The half-blind squirrel stopped chewing and swivelled
   its head
to assess me as another likely patron.

But sensing such jealousy, and need for privacy,
I flinched from competition for the creature's favour;
pulled my collar closer round my throat, kept moving
   down
the avenue of drifting leaves, left them together.

Hospital Flowers

Hospital flowers seem to last longer, or is it only
because they are kept longer, looked at
more often, share the same tainted yet
sustaining air, until like us, they have
become half drugged. Unless the nurses take them
away, day after day they wilt in regulation
vases or commandeered drinking glasses, reminders
of the friends who brought them, and that fear
which, though omnipresent, looms clearer here
than in the world outside, the place where
flowers are forced especially for this purpose.

Those fraying petals, having undergone
the entire process from glossy bud to
insect-like arrest, now appear
as specimens of rare medical aberrations
waiting to be classified. Tulip
and iris, snowdrop and freesia succumb. The inner
delicate brushstrokes fade, the scent disperses.
Anemones harden. As though wincing under a probe,
narcissus, jonquil, and daffodil contract,
twisting around an invisible axis. The trumpets
roll inward – visitors' crumpled sweet-papers.

Yellow and black of pollen powders my fingers
as I rearrange them. And the pattern of veins
marking their tissues, whose colours alter
inevitably as bruises, are like those on the limbs
of flushed, unconscious patients ready to be
wheeled back to their darkened rooms. But though stem

and blossom may soften, the fleshy leaves turn limp
and spongy, still they droop bravely as trophy-flags
or bunting left out in the rain, above the first floor
windows of the plaza, after celebrating
some old local victory again.

House-Guest

Why is it that other peoples' beds always seem
too hard or too soft, and other peoples' food
always too salt or sweet; their houses too cold
(rarely too hot) – never familiar or comfortable?
Is it because as though one skin has gone
(brittle scarf-skin when a scald is finally healing:
the accident that happens away from home),
I am left exposed to every mood of doubt
concerning my validity, more dependent
on smells and textures and shadows and furniture
than the human reassurance of words and friendship.

Yet how quickly we who at first are so unsure
establish new habits and territory, take over
a special corner and stake a claim. How soon
we feel part of the family (and how easily
are disconcerted by an intercepted
glance exchanged between our hosts at such
presumption of familiarity).
Then that skin crackles and splits, the blood beads out
on its shiny rawness, and we clutch at the nearest cloth
to wrap around the wound, even though it may be
an ancient silken robe, their most precious heirloom.

The Gambler

Everything gets thrown in, it's a gamble for
the highest stakes. As if you were a lord and could
dispose of standing timber, family plate, brooches,
horses, portraits, ropes of pearls, ancestral beds
and chairs, finally the house itself – focus
of your future hopes and earliest memories –
all goes under the hammer. The others may object,
but you're the heir. They're helpless. With your
    exorbitant
and reckless nature, to indulge a fraudulent
destructive passion, you seem set on ruination.

Or instead, look at it another way –
as if there's something that makes love and friendship,
every pleasure this world offers (wind and sunlight
on the water, music, books, and growing children,
even health), seem nothing by comparison.
For though you set these tangibilities against
the emptiness that gnaws your spirit, try to count
your blessings, still the need augments. The mysteries
and techniques of the style become your only chance
of satisfaction, the work that might authenticate.

Meanwhile, that trio: loneliness, despair, and boredom,
extend their territory and flaunt their winnings;
gains which must be countered, no matter what the
   price.
For in this gambling palace how decide if you
feel murderous or suicidal when the thousand
flashing crystals of the chandeliers dazzle your burning,
wincing eyes, and other eyes are challenging
and scornful; when this compulsion forces you to
   venture
heart and soul once more, and lures you always further
on towards perfection and away from life.

Always Time

There's always time for making love or
writing poetry – the two
activities revealing certain
parallels. Whether those stories
one has often heard are judged
as more amazing or amusing,
it seems no situation's ever
been too complex or unlikely
or ridiculous to stop
determined people.

Words or phrases sometimes come
with that same urgency, and minutes
open up, allow the time
to seize or lure them (whichever technique
best achieves your purpose); tease them,
mouth them, use them every way
imagination leads, until
enough has passed between them and
yourself, and you feel sure there'll be
a further meeting.

Then, smoothing her hair and skirt,
straightening his tie, they go their separate
ways – return where he had been
before, to what she had been doing;
the prospect of a poem or
an assignation as secure
as such matters ever are –
only the time and place to be
arranged; minds already hard
at work and scheming.

Dreaming

Night after night in that place
I see myself from above,
eyes and back bent to an opened
book, and watch words forming,
the empty pages crawl
with emerging letters like worms.

Only by a tremendous
spasm of will (or is it
a miracle?) – as much
as must have been used to name
the world – can I create
the necessary words.

Impatient and restless as actors
paralysed on the screen
when the mechanism stops,
my characters wait while their speeches
and purposes are imagined.
Not till then can the story continue.

The plots are always violent
and complicated – histories
of the tribe. Like a weary scribe
who copies an unknown language
from a blurred and doubtful source,
I bow over my work,

and wake from such nights strained,
exhausted – not understanding
the obligation to write
each phrase before I read it –
with nothing ever gained or
learned, and the dream forgotten.

Sweet Solitude

Becoming addicted to solitude,
I'm soon helpless with irritation when
away from my room and desk. I prefer
even boredom and despair to anything
except the most extreme stimulation –
my tastes growing coarser and cruder.

Certainly I am becoming cruder
and more direct in refusing whatever
does not please me, in taking only
what I can use, with less show of courtesy,
while cloaked by haughty Byzantine demands
for flagrant luxury and due respect.

But I am not yet confident enough
about this augmenting need, sometimes still
doubt myself, and have urgent relapses
when I believe I shall wither like a
shackled prisoner unless I see someone –
who, doesn't matter – but soon.

In either case I never am satisfied –
always exaggerate, awkward and rude,
or stupidly squander the hours – I must be
the world's greatest sinner: tormented
by being left alone when I want
company, yet deprived of sweet solitude.

Usually Dry-Eyed

'Do you cry easily?' At times. Always
at what is called the cheapest sentiment.
Especially when lovers are reunited,
brothers reconciled, son safe and well
at home with his mother, husband and wife
smiling together. Those are the basic tales.

I'm moved to tears also when the hero wins through
and the siege is lifted, the message delivered, the years
of work rewarded – whenever modest virtue
is recognized. They are tears of pleasure at
the closing of the circle, when Heaven sinks
to earth and existence becomes ordered, just, and perfect.

And tears are brought to my eyes by any report
of natural disaster: when rains fail or fish
move away; devastation destroying the labour of
  hundreds:
sharp-tipped heel crushing the ants' nest.

But tears are not appropriate or adequate
response to the arrogance of cruelty.
Tears make one impotent. Anger is needed. Anger,
the activist. And anger must stay dry-eyed.

Country Lady

Puffy-eyed from sleeping face downward
(as if burrowing into the mattress)
and from too much wine and coffee, not yet
awake, she wanders toward the window,
stares vacantly at grass and preening birds.
Long empty days in the country. Too much
time to suffer the surfeit of time.
Unable to deny the existence of
God, nor sense his hand at work,
how can she mourn him as dead? The dead
god was Eros. Her temperament disbarred
all resurrected substitutes.

Which left her neither lover nor father
as focus. It wasn't mere loss of faith:
that half-expected middle-age crisis.
The old belief in something or other
remained as vaguely inclusive as ever,
but even less rewarding. Now
in the yawning wastes of afternoon,
watching the purposeful birds, she was forced
to admit the limitations
of irony. Only self-consciousness
stiffened against collapse
into abject envy of any devotee.

Not God, not Man. Neither humanist
nor atheist. Disdaining all aid,
or ignorant of the right approach.
Yearning, yet wary of sympathy.
How shall we leave her, this lady, trying
to learn some secret from the evening flight
of birds? What can we hope for her? Better
her life be shattered by revelation,
that some god descend in a fiery Jaguar
while she's tending the roses, than this mostly-
endurable wretchedness and rage?
I wonder if she'll find the answer.

Meat

This subject might be better for a painter,
a moralizing painter – the butcher's window
framing him: anachronistic whiskers,
ruddy face, white coat, striped apron – the sort
of tradesman one had thought no longer could
exist; and her: a proper Chelsea lady
of a certain age, hatted, necklaced,
mackintoshed, whose rouged and powdered cheeks
seemed quite another substance than the flesh
of booted girls who strode along the pavement.

The gloomy afternoon accentuated
all the vivid glitter of the shop:
refrigerator doors, reflecting tiles,
enamel trays displaying cutlets, kidneys,
liver, mince, scallops of veal, oxtails and
stewing steak – that close detail behind which
all the action will take place; and as a
background (filling in for mountains, say,
or distant vista of a plain or lake),
hung carcasses made ghostly by their sheath
of creamy fat, and ghastly by the blood
congealing in their blackened, swollen veins.

He holds a tray of gobbets out for her
inspection almost deferentially,
as though the relics of a martyrdom –
some tortured part – and she bends forward, solemn,
thoughtful, curious. Two faces from
the crowd around the rack or headman's block.

I cannot hear their words, but through the glass,
easy enough to guess he's telling her
how good it is – how tasty, young and fresh.
He vouches for its authenticity.
Those animals were fed the very best
and cossetted. Before their deaths, each one
received its individual injection
of adrenalin, to tenderize
all fibres of the corpse with fear and rage.

She's pondering, bemused, her vacant eye
as bovine as a sphere of gristle, intent
upon deciding what to choose, to make
a really glorious dinner. And in that chrome
and crimson antiseptic antechamber
to the slaughterhouse, they both appear
so absolutely right – the natural focus
of the whole infernal composition.

Aftermath

How many forms of life can clear
a space around themselves, create
a desolation? Only ourselves
and some bacteria – as one
particular incident can cauterize
a zone of memory. Brain
with its dying cells. A whole epoch
lost from the past, scar seared
in the mind, devices of evasion, transference,
or total pull-out – abandonment
of a sector, then re-grouping and counting
survivors: those cells, spores, memories
lucky to have been far enough
from the centre. There was no warning,
no place in this scheme for forethought
or philosophy. And nerve-connections
are made by the same sort of chance
which sets spores floating onto
the agar-plate, or plots the next
appearance of some new mutation,
irresistible virus cutting its swathe
through a population, the forces which empty
a city. Streams of refugees push
up roads and across the countryside:
microbes multiplying in
a Petri dish, organisms liberated
for new purposes, or circuits
overloading, burnt out by
recollection's protective chemistry.

★

Before recovery, the entire
body – physical, political, or astral –
must descend to more primitive levels.

Like a shaman, whose blood is drained away
and set in pans to cool like curds
or gelatine, whose every bone
is disarticulated, moans
and raves to know himself lower than hell,
further than heaven, more helpless
than in the torturer's cave, the courtyard
of the Comneni, the plague-house
or the baby-snatcher's hovel, yet
trusts in his re-integration;
or an astronaut, months out
in space, feeling his identity
stretched like his trajectory
across the constellations, must never
doubt he will at last arrive;
the sufferer can only hope
and wait for an eventual peace.

Whatever its scope, the disaster, private
or global, reaches equilibrium.
Veterans of epidemic,
madness, and war, find their way
back home with faulty limbs and half-gone
memory. And in neglected fields,
self-sown, old strains of wheat,
emmer and spelt, with sparse bristling
heads, show tall against the sky.

The King Must Die

King of this once-splendid country
now falling apart beneath
the blows of my most favoured subjects,
I know how they must feel, wounded
activists, hidden in
a mountain village or a room
behind a garage in the suburbs.

This city, the capital,
stained by blood and noisy with
explosions, has been my brain and heart,
that mountain range the spine to hold
me upright, the river my bloodstream – rocks
and earth and sky as intimate
and vital as my own body.

Somewhere near the palace, in one
of those ministries whose flags are shredded
by bullets, windows shattered, walls
plastered with proclamations, the sons
of murdered deputies argue
with their followers. If this
country is my body, are they
the cells that multiply with jungle
energy, or my true doctors?

I have become just one more man
resigned, amazed, and helpless as
he learns the process of decay:
a miner coughing his lungs out (we
are rich in metals), a forester
watching his leg mortify
where the saw slipped – or a woman after
days of labour, who feels the child
refuse, her last blood pour away.

Like them, and my son's friends (they tell me
he has disappeared), I know
that I am dying with the country
I still love and call myself,
yet have no power or wish to save.

The New Science of Strong Materials

with acknowledgements to Prof. J.E. Gordon, and the 2nd edition of his book, The New Science of Strong Materials, *Penguin, 1976*

Plastic flow or brittle cracking:
whatever the material,
always the inescapable
potentiality within the structure
of either form of fracture –

these two failure mechanisms
are in competition for
all inadequate and earthly matter.
If it yields, the fabric's ductile;
brittle, if at first it cracks.

Trying to visualize the three-
dimensional reality of
imperfection, dislocation's
vortex, the maelstrom of shearing, I guess
the faultlessness and ease with which

the rows of atoms can reject
the slightest deviation, yet not
acknowledge or accept more than
a modicum of individual
involvement or decision.

They barely need do more than shuffle
one small fraction of an Ångström
in position, and quite soon
the incomplete half sheet of atoms
has been edged outside – the others

have combined, closed ranks. Stresses
and strains, pressure and tension: the language
not only of engineering. Though
the combinations seem almost endless,
the basic elements are few,

their governing rules the same: just different
ways of dealing with dislocation
and stopping fracture; rare
recorded attempts and even at times
success at cohesion, bonding, and union.

A Poem

There's a patched-up, incongruous neatness about his
    appearance
like a mongol child who's just had his collar buttoned and
    straightened
and a careless flannel rubbed across his face

Or the photo sent of a hostage, yesterday's newspaper
propped against his chest to prove he's still alive

Or that figure in the witness box, so pale and thin, who
    whatever
the consequence cannot control his grin –
happy to be out of the cellars, to see
other people after months of one ranting examiner –
though his smile reveals the missing teeth; soon
he'll start to say everything he was told, he'll reiterate

And the hostage's wary muffled voice, scratchily taped,
left at the pre-arranged place, will accuse all his
    colleagues

And the child will stumble over his age
and name, but somehow manage a poem.

Two Cripples

Some people manage quite well with one leg,
she said, pouring the coffee, leaning
against the table. They're the lucky ones,
he answered. He was really very nimble.

Most I know drag around
on stumps, or balance a powerful torso
and arms on a little wooden trolley.
And what about those born only with shoulders.

You're changing the subject, she countered. I'm talking
about cripples, how they adjust
and learn to use crutches. Alone in the kitchen,
they both seemed absolutely normal.

One leg, that's nothing, he insisted. Peg-leg.
Sounds almost jolly. It could be much worse.
Who isn't crippled, one way or the other.
Imagine always walking on stilts.

The Dancing Floor

Is this the thread? Have I found Ariadne?
Will the Minotaur trample me down
in the stench and dark of the labyrinth;

can my luck hold and let me reach
the centre, meet and kill the monster,
Ariadne's slobbering half-brother?

Such precedents. She betrayed her father –
but that was not enough to stop
Theseus. He abandoned her.

Then he forgot to change the sail
to white from black – in his turn caused
a father's grief and death. Where

to end the tale? Before Phaedra
and Hippolytus, or after?
One action leads inexorably

to the next: victims of the gods,
their own passions, or types of cunning
and vainglorious will? I do not know

if Ariadne died at Naxos,
or married Dionysius – and thus
escaped the family drama; nor why

I must accept the risk, and trust
this clue will lead me straight into
the maze's core, the sacred dancing-floor,

where Ariadne, Theseus, Minotaur,
triumphant in their unity,
wait to welcome a new partner.